SECOND EDITION

GOOD PICTURES BAD PICTURES

Porn-Proofing Today's Young Kids

Kristen A. Jenson, MA

illustrated by Debbie Fox

A NOTE FROM THE AUTHOR

I'm happy to introduce a second edition of *Good Pictures Bad Pictures*! Important revisions to the main text clarify and update scientific information and improve the arguments against pornography. I've also added "Let's Talk!" questions at the end of the chapters--a great way to deepen and solidify understanding. The *Tips for Parents and Caregivers* section was completely rewritten based on my best advice after years of study and feedback from parents and professionals. Finally, the interior typography and design was improved to make it easier to read, and the cover design was updated to reflect the popularity of mobile devices. Here are some great tips for using this new edition!

FIVE TIPS FOR USING GOOD PICTURES BAD PICTURES

1. Go at your own pace. Read it one chapter at a time or the entire book at once—it's up to you and your child. I encourage you to remember it's never a "one and done" conversation when it comes to protecting kids from porn.

2. Encourage questions. Discussing the "Let's Talk!" questions after each chapter will help to deepen your child's understanding. Of course, kids often come up with their own questions, and some are doozies! If one stumps you, it's OK to say, "That's a great question! Let me think about it and get back with you."

3. Use your own stories and vocabulary. Feel free to expand upon analogies or use stories from your own family to clarify concepts. This book is *your* tool—*you* decide how best to use it!

4. Remain calm. If your child reveals a past exposure to pornography, take a breath and listen. See this as a sign of trust and a good opportunity to find out (possibly over several conversations) how much they've been exposed to, where it happened and who they were with.

5. Grab your FREE companion poster or guide by texting **GPGIFT to 44222** or visiting www.GPBP.info. Also, don't miss the ***Tips for Parents and Caregivers*** in the back of this book.

A SPECIAL STORY ABOUT THE ILLUSTRATIONS

Ten years before I started this book project, my young son passed away. A few months after his death, Debbie Fox brought me a beautiful watercolor portrait of him. She had painted it from the photo on the back of his memorial service program. I count this gift as one of my greatest treasures.

When I asked myself the question, "How do I illustrate a book to help children reject pornography?" I knew I wanted the illustrations to be in watercolor. They needed to be classic and soft to counter the harshness of pornography; and real, not cartoonish—I didn't want to risk trivializing this serious problem.

It was a no-brainer that Debbie was the one to paint the authentic and beautiful illustrations we needed, and I'm grateful she accepted the challenge. She was a dream to work with, showing endless patience and flexibility. I believe her hand-painted artistry makes *Good Pictures Bad Pictures* an even more comfortable and inviting book for parents and kids.

CONTENTS

Chapter 1: What's Pornography?   1

Chapter 2: What's an Addiction?   7

Chapter 3: My Feeling Brain   11

Chapter 4: My Thinking Brain   15

Chapter 5: My Two Brains Work Together   19

Chapter 6: My Brain's Attraction Center   23

Chapter 7: How Pornography Tricks the Brain into an Addiction   27

Chapter 8: My Thinking Brain's CAN DO Plan!   31

Chapter 9: I Can Escape the Poison of Pornography   39

Glossary of Key Terms   46

Tips for Parents and Caregivers   47

More Tools to Protect Kids!   48

CHAPTER 1

WHAT'S PORNOGRAPHY?

One Sunday afternoon, Mom and I sat on the couch and flipped through a pile of photo albums. I liked looking at pictures from our trip to the beach last summer and Uncle Mike's wedding last fall.

After we finished, Mom got a serious look on her face.

"There's something I've wanted to talk with you about," Mom said. "Our photo album is full of *good pictures* that remind us of how important our family and friends are. But did you know there are *bad pictures*, too?"

I shook my head. "What do you mean by *bad pictures*?"

Mom closed the photo album and looked at me. "The bad pictures I'm talking about are called **pornography** or *porn*."

"What's poor-nog-gra-fee?" I asked.

"Pornography means pictures, videos, shows or even cartoons of people with little or no clothes on. Have you ever seen pictures like that?" Mom asked.

I thought about it and then I remembered something.

"I once saw a picture of a naked man and woman in a science book at the library. All of their parts were labeled. Is that pornography?"

Mom smiled. "No, there's a difference between a drawing in a science book and pornography."

She opened up the photo album and pointed to pictures of me and my cousins at the beach.

"Pornography shows the parts of the body that we keep private—like the parts we cover with a swimsuit. Every part of our body is good, including our private parts, but taking pictures of them and showing them to others is not good. It's important for your safety to keep private parts private."

For a moment, Mom stopped to think.

"Most kids who see pornography know immediately that it feels wrong or weird. Some kids say it makes them feel embarrassed or even sick to their stomach."

"Then why do kids look at it?" I asked.

"Pornography is tricky because it's designed to feel exciting to your body. In fact, pornography tricks the brain into releasing a big dose of **chemicals** that make your body feel really good—for a short time. But tricking the brain with pornography can soon lead to big problems."

Mom gently tapped the top of my head with her finger.

"The problem is that pornography can hurt parts of your growing brain. Looking at pornography is dangerous."

"Mom, if it's so dangerous, how do kids find it?"

"Many kids see it by accident on computers, phones, tablets or other devices. Sometimes kids are shown pornography by another person— even by a friend or family member. Has that ever happened to you?"

I shook my head. "No."

"I'm glad. No one should ever show pornography to a child. If that ever happens, will you come and tell me? I promise you won't get into trouble. It's just really important for me to know so I can help you protect yourself."

"Sure, Mom . . . but I still don't understand why anyone would want to look at pornography."

Mom thought for a minute.

"It's normal for kids to be curious, and some kids are curious about pornography. For many kids, wanting to see pornography can feel like the pull of a giant magnet. After they see only one pornographic picture, their brains can be tricked into wanting to see more and more."

Mom put her hands on my shoulders and looked me in the eye.

"Part of my job is to warn you about danger. I've taught you to wear a helmet when you ride your bike to protect your brain on the *outside*. But pornography gets *inside* your brain and hurts it. Do you want to protect your brain on the inside, too?"

"I guess so. But how can pornography hurt my brain?"

"I can think of at least three ways. First, pornography teaches that a person's body is an object to *use* instead of a whole person who deserves to be loved and respected. When people see others as objects, it's a lot easier to treat them badly, isn't it?"

"I guess so. I mean, objects don't have feelings but people do!"

"You're right! And that leads us to the second reason pornography is harmful. It teaches lies! A lot of pornography shows people being mean and acting like it's fun. Do you think hurting others is a good way to have fun?"

"No way," I said.

Mom smiled and put her arm around my shoulders.

"But that's not all. The third way pornography can hurt a person's brain is that looking at it can become a bad habit or even a serious **addiction**. I want to teach you more about addiction so *you* can protect *your* brain from addictions of all kinds."

LET'S TALK!

Pornography means harmful pictures of people with little or no clothing on. Looking at it can cause two opposite feelings at the same time. Viewing pornography is dangerous because it can hurt my brain in at least three ways. One of them is addiction.

Why is it important to keep private parts private?

_____

_____

What different feelings can seeing pornography cause?

_____

_____

What are the three ways pornography can hurt my brain?

_____

_____

Notes:

_____

_____

_____

_____

CHAPTER 2

WHAT'S AN ADDICTION?

"Do you know what an *addiction* is?" Mom asked.

I pointed to a brownie sundae on the front cover of Mom's magazine. "Aunt Amy says she's addicted to chocolate," I said with a grin.

Mom smiled. "Some people joke about addictions, but a real addiction is a very serious problem."

Mom's eyebrows scrunched together, and she thought for a minute.

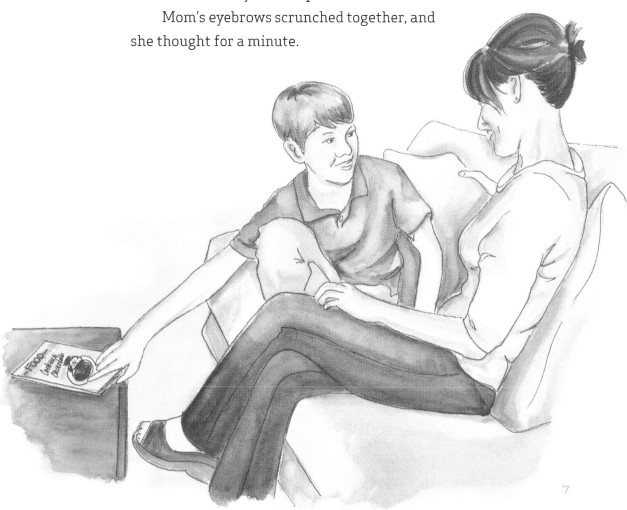

"An addiction is like a powerful habit that is so strong most people who suffer with an addiction feel they can't quit—even when they have tried really hard to stop. It feels like a trap they can't escape from."

"I remember Grandma used to smoke cigarettes. Was she addicted?" I asked.

"Yes, she was. It took her many years to quit smoking. Other members of our family have struggled with addictions to alcohol or other drugs. But people can also become addicted to behaviors like gambling or looking at pornography."

"Wow, people can really become addicted to looking at bad pictures?"

"It's true. Some people become addicted more easily than others. But you *never* want to become addicted to anything, if you can help it."

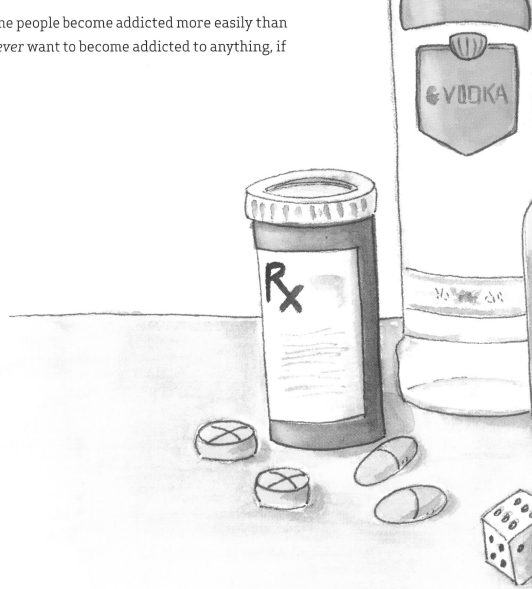

"Why? What happens?"

"Most people with addictions make bad choices that end up hurting themselves and the people they love. They often try to hide their addiction by lying to their friends and family. As they become more and more addicted, they can lose interest in their relationships, school, or even having fun."

Mom sighed. "It's so important to protect your brain! Most people find it really hard to get better from an addiction."

"Why is it so hard? Can't you just stop if you want to?"

"It's not that easy, and it all has to do with your two brains."

"Wait—I have *two* brains?"

Mom chuckled. "Actually, you only have one brain, but there are two major parts to your brain that are involved in addiction. Let's call them the **feeling brain** and the **thinking brain**. Learning about your two brains can help protect you from addiction."

LET'S TALK!

People can become addicted to behaviors like gambling and pornography as well as substances like drugs and alcohol. An addiction is like being trapped in a very bad habit. People with addictions often make poor choices and lie to cover up their addiction. Addiction involves both the feeling brain and the thinking brain.

What is an addiction?

_____

_____

What kinds of things can people become addicted to?

_____

_____

Why are addictions harmful?

_____

_____

_____

Notes:

_____

_____

_____

_____

CHAPTER 3

MY FEELING BRAIN

Mom stood and picked up her tablet. She tapped the screen until she found a picture of the human brain. We sat down at our kitchen counter to look at it.

Mom pointed at the picture. "Your feeling brain is right here in the center. It has several parts that work *automatically* to keep

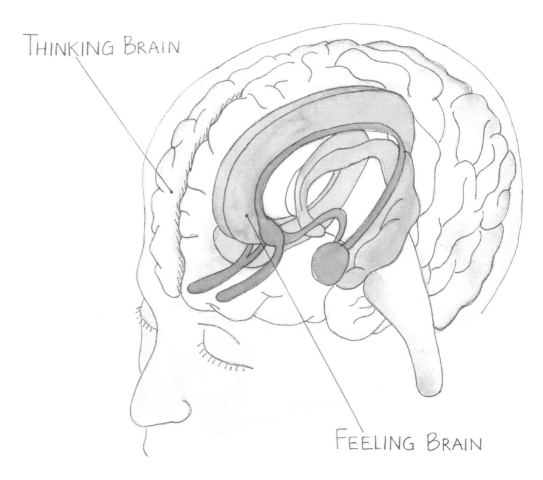

THINKING BRAIN

FEELING BRAIN

you alive. For example, when you go out to play on a very hot day, what happens?"

"I get sweaty."

"Right! That's your feeling brain sending a message to your body to help it cool down.

"What about when you go outside on a cold day without a jacket on?" she asked.

"I start to shiver."

"Exactly! That's your feeling brain sending a message to help your body warm up!"

"Your feeling brain is also in charge of basic **drives** that keep you alive. For example, the feeling brain makes you feel hungry and thirsty so you'll want to eat and get enough to drink. It has a special **reward system** that gives you a feeling of *pleasure* for

doing things, like eating, that help you survive."

"That must be why I like ice cream so much!"

Mom smiled. "Rewarding you with pleasure for doing important things is a big part of the feeling brain's job. Your feeling brain is necessary for your survival, but it also needs your help."

"Why?" I wondered.

"Because your feeling brain doesn't know right from wrong. It's kind of like a cheetah hunting a gazelle. Cheetahs kill gazelles for food—for them, it's not a matter of right or wrong, it's their survival instinct to kill when they're hungry.

"But humans are different from animals," Mom explained. "Humans have the ability to *think* about what they're doing, rather than always acting on their *feelings*."

"So the thinking brain is like a mom who tells a kid to stop eating too much ice cream," I joked.

"Exactly!" Mom winked, and we laughed together.

LET'S TALK!

My feeling brain is in charge of keeping my body alive. It makes me hungry, thirsty, and keeps my body at the right temperature. My feeling brain makes me want what it believes I need and then rewards me with feelings of pleasure for repeating those actions. But it's got one big weakness: it doesn't know right from wrong.

What three important jobs does the feeling brain do?

How does the feeling brain help keep me alive?

What's the feeling brain's biggest weakness?

Notes:

CHAPTER 4

MY THINKING BRAIN

Mom tapped me on my forehead with her finger.

"This part of your brain, right here in front, is your *thinking* brain. It helps you solve problems, like doing your math homework or figuring out how to build a fort. Your thinking brain can make plans and exercise self-control, like when you control your temper. But more importantly, your thinking brain can learn *right from wrong*. It can learn how to make *good* choices because it remembers the consequences of *bad* choices. Your thinking brain can help you to stop, think, and make good decisions."

Mom pointed to a drawing of the thinking brain.

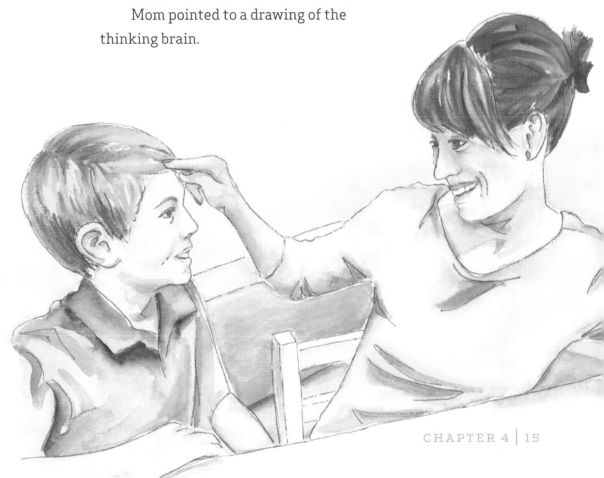

"Can you think of something your thinking brain helps you to do?" Mom asked.

I thought hard.

"Well, I've learned not to hit my brother when I get mad at him."

Mom smiled.

"Right. You're getting good at controlling your anger because your thinking brain has learned to stop and remember the bad consequences of hitting your brother."

"Can my thinking brain keep me from getting an addiction?"

"Yes. Every time you decide to make a good choice, your thinking brain becomes stronger so it can protect you from things like addiction. It's almost like exercising a muscle—the more you work it, the stronger it gets."

I flexed my arm. "I had no idea my brain can get strong like a muscle!"

Mom leaned over and hugged me. "You're getting stronger every time you make a good decision!"

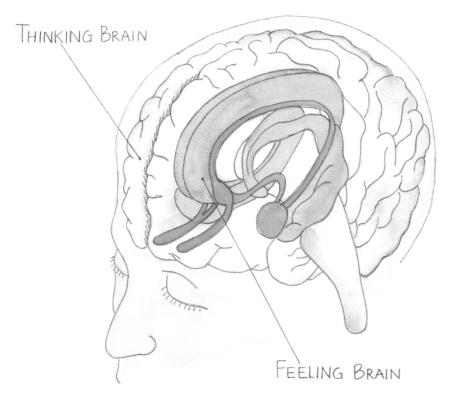

THINKING BRAIN

FEELING BRAIN

LET'S TALK!

My thinking brain helps me solve problems, use self-control, and make smart choices between right and wrong, good and bad. By exercising my thinking brain, I can make it stronger and protect my brain from addiction!

What three important jobs does the thinking brain do?

_____

_____

How can I make my thinking brain stronger?

_____

_____

Notes:

_____

_____

_____

_____

_____

_____

_____

CHAPTER 5

MY TWO BRAINS WORK TOGETHER

om stood up, and we walked over to a window that looked out onto our street.

"I'll give you an example of how both brains can work together. Let's pretend it's a hot summer afternoon and you're very hungry. An ice cream truck pulls up on the other side of our street."

She put up her left fist.

"Here's your feeling brain. It wants to eat, so it says, 'Go get the ice cream *right now!*'"

Mom put up her right hand. "But your thinking brain says, 'Stop! Look for cars first!'"

Mom brought her hands together, with her right hand covering her left fist.

"With your thinking brain in charge, your two brains can work together to keep you safe *and* help you get what you want. But what do you think happens if an addiction weakens your thinking brain so your feeling brain takes over making all the decisions?"

I thought for a minute.

"Well, I might run out into the street and get hit by a car... because I wouldn't *think* to look both ways."

"Right. Without your thinking brain, your feeling

brain would do whatever it wants, even if it's not safe for you. So which brain needs to stay in charge of making decisions?"

"My thinking brain!"

"Exactly." Mom nodded.

"Mom, all this talk about ice cream has got *both* my brains wanting some!" I laughed.

Mom smiled. "How about after dinner? You can help me get it ready, and then we'll talk more about keeping our brains safe from addiction and pornography."

I wanted some ice cream right away, but I used my thinking brain to help me wait until after dinner.

LET'S TALK!

Both of my brains are important. But as I grow up, I need to make sure my thinking brain is in charge because my feeling brain doesn't stop to think before acting. I can stay safe and make good choices by keeping my thinking brain in charge.

Which of my two brains can make better decisions? Why?

_____

_____

_____

How do my thinking brain and feeling brain work together?

_____

_____

_____

How can I keep my thinking brain in charge?

_____

_____

_____

Notes: _____

_____

_____

_____

_____

CHAPTER 6

MY BRAIN'S ATTRACTION CENTER

After dinner, Mom and I sat eating our ice cream at the kitchen table.

After I finished my last spoonful, Mom asked, "Did you know that some people think a pornography addiction is harder to overcome than a drug addiction?"

"Really? Why?"

"Because pornography fires up one of the most *powerful* parts of the feeling brain called the **attraction center**."

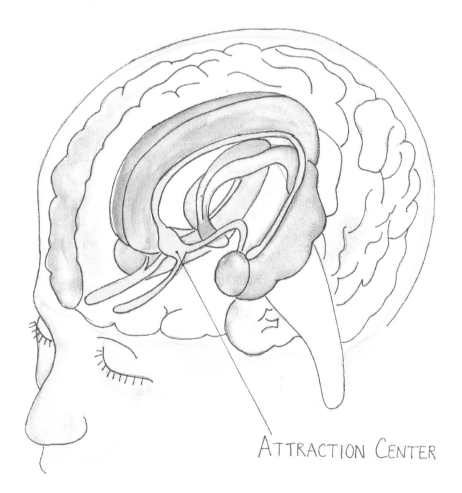

ATTRACTION CENTER

"The attraction center?"

Mom tapped on her tablet again and pointed to a part of the brain diagram.

"Everyone has an attraction center; it's part of the feeling brain. It's normally turned off in young kids until they get older. The attraction center creates feelings of excitement and happiness that lead people to fall in love. It makes them want to be close to one another."

I rolled my eyes. "So why is *that* so important?"

Mom tousled my hair.

"Without the brain's attraction center, moms and dads wouldn't be attracted to each other or want to get married. And if they didn't fall in love and come together, they wouldn't have babies. And if they didn't have babies, the human race might not survive . . . which means *you* wouldn't be here today!"

"Well, I guess that *is* important." I grinned.

"It's also important to remember that pornography tricks people into believing lies."

"You mean lies about how people should treat each other?"

"That's right! Watching pornography can lead you to believe that people are objects to *use* instead of human beings to *love*. Everyone has feelings and deserves to be treated with kindness, so showing people as objects is just one way pornography lies to people who look at it."

"Don't people know the pictures aren't real? How can it hurt to watch people who are just acting?"

"Good question. The attraction center is designed to bring *real* people together, but it can't tell the difference between a picture and a real person. Looking at pornography *tricks* the brain into turning on very powerful feelings that are difficult to control, especially for kids. And that can become a big problem."

Mom picked up my brother's toy race car from off the floor. "Pretend this car is real. The *gas pedal* is like the attraction center. The *brakes* are like the thinking brain. What would happen if you pushed the gas pedal to the floor *and* the brakes weren't working?"

"I would crash and get hurt."

"Right. Pornography is dangerous because viewing it can put the feeling brain in charge of driving *you*, way before your thinking brain has strong enough brakes to control those feelings of attraction. And that can lead to developing an out-of-control addiction."

Mom handed me the race car. "So what are *you* going to do if you run into bad pictures?"

"I'm going to protect my brain by not looking at pornography."

Mom smiled again and put her arm around my shoulders. "You should be proud of yourself for making such good choices!"

LET'S TALK!

My attraction center is part of my feeling brain. It's extremely powerful because it has a very important job—to bring moms and dads together to create families. But pornography can trick my attraction center and turn it on too early, before my thinking brain has the brakes to control it. That's why I need to turn away from bad pictures.

What job does the attraction center do?

_____

_____

How does pornography trick the attraction center?

_____

_____

Why is it important for me to stay away from bad pictures?

_____

_____

Notes:_____

_____

_____

CHAPTER 7

HOW PORNOGRAPHY TRICKS THE BRAIN INTO AN ADDICTION

Mom and I got up from the table and worked together doing the dishes.

"Mom, do you think a kid could get addicted after seeing only one bad picture?"

"Most kids won't," Mom said. "But some kids who are not

prepared to reject it might get hooked very quickly."

"How does that happen so fast?"

"I'll try to explain. Pornography tricks the brain into releasing a big dose of chemicals that make the person watching it feel good, at least for a while. The scary thing about a pornography addiction is that the brain is tricked into making too much of its own drug!"

"Really?"

"Yes. Many scientists now believe that looking at pornography can affect the brain in the same way as taking a strong drug. Brain scans show that using pornography may even shrink part of the thinking brain!"

"That's scary!"

"It is! You already know never to use illegal or harmful drugs, but in some ways pornography can be worse. Although a drug addiction is very hard to overcome, at least the body has a way of getting rid of the drugs within a few days. Unlike drugs in the body, the brain can't get rid of pornography. Once you see those shocking pictures, they can always be there for you to remember."

"That's not fair!"

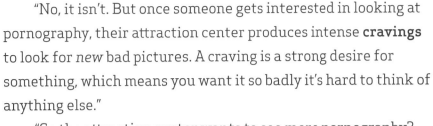

"No, it isn't. But once someone gets interested in looking at pornography, their attraction center produces intense **cravings** to look for *new* bad pictures. A craving is a strong desire for something, which means you want it so badly it's hard to think of anything else."

"So the attraction center wants to see more pornography? Why?"

"Because the brain gets bored with old stuff and excited by new stuff. Do you remember the last time you got excited about something *new*?"

"That's easy! My remote control truck I just bought. It took me a long time to save up for that!"

"Good example!" Mom said with a smile. "Now, do you remember when something new became kind of boring?"

I reminded Mom about the Crime Buster Detective Kit I got last year. I dreamed about it for weeks before my birthday, but now I almost never play with it.

Mom nodded. "It's the same with pornography. When pictures become boring, people look for even more shocking pictures and videos in order to feel the same level of excitement they did at first. Searching for new pornographic pictures and videos is what feeds an addiction."

"Wow! I don't want to get an addiction!"

"Me neither. The problem is that seeing pornography creates a feeling of excitement in your body very quickly, even before you can turn away. It takes less than a half second. And seeing even one picture can lead a kid to be super curious about pornography. The good thing is that *you can choose* to put the brakes on those feelings of excitement and curiosity *before* they grow into an addiction."

"How?"

"Great question!" Mom tapped the front of her head. "Your thinking brain can do it—it just needs a plan!"

LET'S TALK!

Memories of pornography can lead to intense cravings to see more pictures or videos. But the brain can quickly become bored. An addiction gets started when people search for new and more intense pornography in order to get their attraction center excited. To avoid an addiction, the thinking brain needs a plan.

How is an addiction to pornography the same as an addiction to drugs?

How is an addiction to pornography different from an addiction to drugs?

How does an addiction grow and get worse?

Notes:

CHAPTER 8

MY THINKING BRAIN'S CAN DO PLAN!

Mom said I should do my very best to stay away from pornography. But if I ever come across pornography, here's what I **CAN DO**.

These are the steps I take as soon as I see a bad picture or video:

Close my eyes.

Always tell a trusted adult.

Name it when I see it.

Whenever a bad picture pops up in my mind, I practice these important skills:

Distract myself with something different.

Order my thinking brain to be the boss!

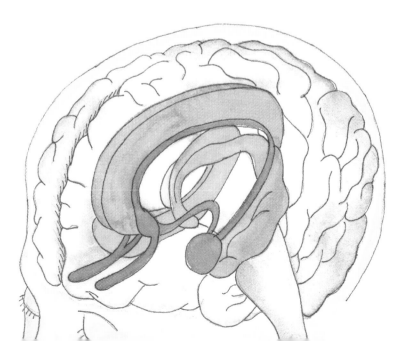

CLOSE MY EYES IMMEDIATELY.

Seconds count with bad pictures, and the longer I look, the stronger the memory becomes. After I close my eyes, I can *turn away*. If I'm on the internet, I can turn off my device without looking at the screen. Turning it off is better than trying to close the website.

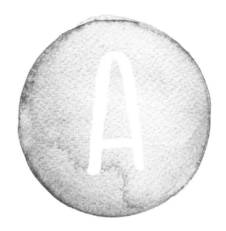

ALWAYS TELL A TRUSTED ADULT.

Keeping pornography a secret is never a good idea. That's why I need to tell a trusted adult right away *every time* I see a bad picture. Mom says the bad image may actually bother me more if I keep it to myself.

If it's too hard to talk about, I can always leave a note. That way my mom or dad will know to find a time when we can talk.

And if I'm ever at a place where someone shows me pornography, I can use a secret code phrase (like "my stomach feels strange") to alert my mom or dad to come and get me.

NAME IT WHEN I SEE IT.

Say quietly, but out loud, "That's pornography!" whenever I see a bad picture, video, or cartoon. Naming it helps my thinking brain to know what it is and reject it.

Our family has decided to help each other recognize pornography when we see it. Even if we're out in public, we can quietly whisper to each other, "That's pornography!"

DISTRACT MYSELF.

When an image is bothering me, I can distract myself with something different that is really exciting or interesting to me. I can also distract myself by doing something physical, like riding my bike, taking the dog for a walk, or playing a fun game with a friend.

Mom told me that some kids recite an encouraging poem, sing a fun song, or, if they follow a faith tradition, say a prayer or repeat a passage of scripture to get their minds turned away from pornography.

I can train my thinking brain to focus on something different* whenever a bad picture pops up in my thoughts. I can choose to pay attention to something else. With *practice*, those bad pictures will bother me less and less.

*Please refer to *Tips for Parents and Caregivers* at the back of this book for more help on "forgetting" bad pictures.

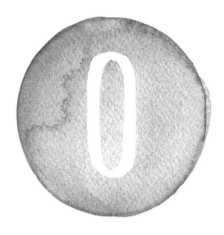

ORDER MY THINKING BRAIN TO BE THE BOSS!

I can decide to never, ever go looking for more pornography, even after I've been exposed to it. A good way to order my thinking brain to be the boss is to make it *talk* to my feeling brain, like this:

"Feeling brain, you may be curious to see more bad pictures, but I can choose to use my thinking brain to stay free from pornography."

I CAN DO this! I can make my thinking brain strong by deciding not to view pornography and by learning to control my thoughts.

MY CAN DO PLAN

 **C** Close my eyes immediately.

 **A** Always tell a trusted adult.

 **N** Name it when I see it.

 **D** Distract myself.

 **O** Order my thinking brain to be the boss!

LET'S TALK!

Because pornography is tricky and might take me by surprise, I need a plan. I can do the first three steps of the CAN DO Plan any time I see a bad picture. Whenever a memory of pornography pops back up in my mind, I can practice the last two skills to help me focus on something else and keep my brain safe!

Why is it important to close my eyes immediately when I see a bad picture?

_____

Who are the trusted adults I can talk to when I see a bad picture?

_____

How does naming a bad picture by saying, "That's pornography!" help me to use my thinking brain?

_____

What specific activity can I do or think about doing when a bad picture pops up in my mind?

_____

What can I say to help keep my thinking brain in charge?

_____

CHAPTER 9

I CAN ESCAPE THE POISON OF PORNOGRAPHY

The next day after dinner, Dad and I hurried into the garage to work on my bike.

"Hey, I heard you and Mom were talking yesterday about *bad pictures*."

"They're called *pornography*, Dad."

Dad smiled. "Well, your mom's right—porn is bad for the brain."

He picked up a wrench, and we started working on my bike. After we finished adding a new seat and handles, it looked brand-new!

"Thanks, Dad, it looks awesome!"

I took my bike for a ride and then came whizzing back and parked it in the garage. After we put away our tools, Dad pulled out a box from a locked cabinet and held it out for me to see.

"Do you know what this is?" he asked.

I looked at the label. "Is it poison?"

"Yes, it is. These chunks of bait are very tasty to rats, and they mistake them for food. But after a few bites, the poison begins to kill them."

Dad put the poison back into the cabinet and locked it shut.

"Pornography is a lot like poisonous bait. In fact, people who sell pornography put it on the internet, TV, signs, and in magazines to try to trick you. At first, pornography might seem like a good idea because it can feel so exciting to your body and brain. But soon, it can damage your brain, a lot like a poison."

"Mom said that if I ever see bad pictures, I need to say, 'That's pornography!' and then get away from it fast."

"That's right. If the rats could say, 'That's poison!' and then run away from it, do you think it could hurt them?"

"No, I guess not."

"If you recognize the pornography bait as the poison that it is and stay away from it, you'll be able to keep your brain safe."

Dad gave me a big hug.

"Remember our saying: If you make good choices *today*..."

"Good things will happen tomorrow!" I chimed in. I'd heard Dad say that a thousand times, and we both laughed.

"Anytime you want to talk, I'm here for you, okay?"

"Thanks, Dad."

Mom opened the door and smiled. "Hey, let me take a picture of you two with your latest project."

Mom's camera clicked and flashed.

Dad opened the kitchen door for us and turned off the garage lights. "Come on. I don't know about you, but I'm ready for dessert."

A pan of warm brownies sat on the kitchen table, and we all took turns sliding them out with a spatula.

Mom showed us the photos she'd taken of me and Dad.

Mom smiled. "These are *good pictures* to add to our family photo album. They'll make great memories."

As I looked at the photo of Dad and me, I knew that *this* was the kind of picture I wanted to have in *my* brain.

When it comes to pornography, I want to be in control by using my thinking brain. And now I know I CAN DO it.

LET'S TALK!

Pornography is like picture poison for the brain. I can choose to look for good pictures that help me love and respect others. I can reject bad pictures that turn people into objects and can lead to an addiction. I can always reject pornography if I use my thinking brain.

How is pornography like poisonous bait for my brain?

How can I have more control of the pictures I put in my brain?

What can I do or remember if I feel curious to look at bad pictures?

Notes:

GLOSSARY OF KEY TERMS

Addiction: An addiction is a chronic disease of the brain's reward system. A dysfunctional reward system creates strong cravings for the addictive substance or behavior, which cause addicts to lose control and compulsively seek it out despite negative consequences. Addicts develop tolerance, so they require more intense levels of stimulation for satisfaction, and they experience withdrawal if they cannot use their addictive drug or engage in their addictive behavior. Most addicts experience cycles of relapse and remission. Without treatment, addictions are progressive and can result in disability or premature death.

Attraction Center: The structures of the brain involved in sexual attraction and arousal.

Chemicals: Substances made of tiny parts called atoms and molecules. The chemicals in the brain are like signals that carry messages from one part of the brain to another.

Cravings: Cravings are strong desires. More than a hunger, a craving is a powerful longing for something specific. Cravings can be so overwhelming that they wake addicts up during the night from a sound sleep.

Drive: A powerful need or instinct that motivates behavior, like hunger or sexual desire.

Feeling Brain: The limbic region of the brain responsible for our emotions as well as our survival instincts and feelings of pleasure. Memory and learning are also involved with the limbic system.

Pornography: (Simple definition) Pornography means pictures, videos, or even cartoons of people with little or no clothes on. (Advanced definition) Any kind of media—like pictures, videos, songs, or stories—that is designed to arouse sexual feelings by showing nudity or sexual behavior.

Reward System: The parts of the brain involved in creating feelings of pleasure or satisfaction to reward behaviors important for survival. An addiction corrupts the reward system so that it rewards addictive behaviors that are not helpful for survival.

Thinking Brain: This area of the brain is called the prefrontal cortex and is responsible for putting the brakes on the appetites of the limbic system. The prefrontal cortex learns right from wrong and can make plans and solve problems. It may shrink in size as the addiction transfers strength and control to the limbic system. A few ways to fortify the prefrontal cortex include focused meditation, exercising self-discipline, and acting on plans to achieve goals.

TIPS FOR PARENTS AND CAREGIVERS

Talking with kids about pornography may seem daunting, but it's totally doable! The good news is that when children are prepared to reject pornography, they CAN DO it! Here are some of my best tips!

1. Become your child's go-to expert! Teach your kids to ask *you* instead of their friends or the internet when they have a question or hear a word they don't understand—many kids get pulled into porn when they search for the definitions of sexualized slang.

2. Remember that children are not bad if they are intrigued by pornography. It's biologically normal for kids to want to see nude pictures. It's not shameful to be curious—but it can be dangerous. Use kindness to educate and persuade your child to take good care of their brain and body by turning away from pornography.

3. Teach your child how to "forget" bad pictures. Pornography makes very powerful memories in a child's mind! That's why young kids need their parent's help. "Forgetting" or neutralizing a pornographic image is simple but takes practice and guidance. Essentially, a child needs a plan to create a new neural pathway away from the memory of pornography. Here's how:

- Help your child identify a fun or exciting activity they love. Maybe it's a song, a funny part of a movie, a toy, or a physical activity. It can be anything they enjoy that helps to distract them.

- Teach your child to think about that special activity whenever a bad picture pops up in their mind. Doing something physical that requires mental concentration can also help distract a child from focusing on the memory of the bad picture.

- Encourage your child to keep practicing. At first, their mind will naturally return to the strong memory of pornography. That's OK. Every time that happens, ask them to think of their special fun activity. It will take practice, but as they work at it, the bad memory will pop up less frequently and have less power over their mind.

4. Begin explaining sex earlier rather than later. Although I designed this book so it can be read to kids before the "sex talks," I highly recommend beginning layered conversations from a young age. The earlier you start, the more comfortable these conversations will be! *Today's parents are competing with the porn industry for influence over the sexual templates of their children.* Teach kids what you believe is the purpose of sex before the porn industry poisons their minds with violence, rape scenes, child abuse, and other degrading acts. If your kids feel comfortable asking *you* questions about sex, they'll be that much more resilient against pornography..

5. Teach kids never to take or share pictures of themselves without their clothes on. Sharing nudes (sexting) is a growing trend and even young children are being "sextorted" online to share nude photos and videos. Let's teach kids to reject this practice before it even starts!

6. Continue to mentor your child with regular conversations. Take the first step by reading this book to your child, and each step after that will be much easier. Help your kids develop an *internal* filter by using the CAN DO Plan to avoid addiction. Each talk will build their trust. Each conversation will increase their safety.

You've got this! I invite you to join our community at **ProtectYoungMinds.org**, on Instagram, and in our Protect Young Minds Facebook Let's Talkaa group. Week after week we'll support you as you face the challenges of raising your amazing child in the digital age.

MORE TOOLS TO PROTECT KIDS!

Check out ProtectYoungMinds.org

Real, ongoing support to help parents mentor kids in the digital age:

- **Up-to-date information** on prevention strategies and new threats.

- **Community.** Let's Talk parent discussion group on Facebook. You're not alone!

- **Free** downloadable guides and posters.

- **Help from experts** and therapists to answer your toughest questions.

- **Constant encouragement.** You can do this!

Help Protect Your Child's Classmates!

We've developed a multi-media rich curriculum based on the principles in *Good Pictures Bad Pictures!*

Go to ProtectYoungMinds.org/curriculum to learn more and request that this course be taught in your child's school. No child deserves to face the porn industry alone!

Jr. Version for ages 3-7

Good Pictures Bad Pictures Jr. makes it easy for parents to protect their young kids. Using gentle, age-appropriate messages, children will learn to **Turn, Run & Tell** when they are accidentally exposed to inappropriate content. The Jr. version empowers young kids with their **first internal filter**!

More Translations of *Good Pictures Bad Pictures*

Available in **Spanish**, **German** and **Chinese**! Find out more at ProtectYoungMinds.org/books

EMAIL: info@ProtectYoungMinds.org
WEB: www.ProtectYoungMinds.org

ABOUT THE AUTHOR AND ILLUSTRATOR

KRISTEN A. JENSON

Kristen is a best-selling author, the CEO of Glen Cove Press LLC, and the founder of ProtectYoungMinds.org, a website dedicated to empowering parents to teach their kids to reject pornography. She holds a BA in English Literature and an MA in Organizational Communication.

DEBBIE FOX

Debbie holds a bachelor's degree from Brigham Young University where she started as an art major and has continued her art education through community classes. She illustrated the new *Good Pictures Bad Pictures Jr.: A Simple Plan to Protect Young Minds* with her authentic water color paintings.

Thank You!

It takes a village to produce a book like this! The writings and online video presentations of Donald L. Hilton Jr., MD, helped me explain how the brain can develop an actual addiction to pornography. Specifically, I shared and expanded upon his "ice cream truck" analogy in chapter 5. Special recognition goes to Jill Manning, PhD, author of *What's the Big Deal about Pornography? A Guide for the Internet Generation*. Her work inspired the first four of the CAN DO Plan strategies listed in chapter 8. The videos on YourBrainOnPorn.com and others by Gordon S. Bruin, MA, LPC were instrumental in creating simple, kid-friendly explanations of our two brains. Claudine Gallacher, MA, spent hundreds of hours serving as a research assistant and writing coach; her encouragement and feedback were crucial contributions. My friends, Jared and Nicole Liebert and their sons, served as models for the illustrations and were early and enthusiastic "guinea pig" readers. I am grateful for all the encouragement I received from my writing group, The Columbia River Writers, and author Tanya Parker Mills, who helped me start my blog, Protect Young Minds. The dozens of parents who served as volunteer test-readers gave critical feedback that helped me improve and make this book more effective for kids. Debbie Fox and Evan MacDonald brought this book to life with their artistry and skills. I am deeply grateful to everyone who helped me to write and publish *Good Pictures Bad Pictures*!

PRAISE FOR *GOOD PICTURES BAD PICTURES*

"*Good Pictures Bad Pictures* is the practical, positive, and powerful tool families need. I whole-heartedly recommend reading this with your children regularly so they will develop self-control—the ultimate protection from pornography."

VAUNA DAVIS, FOUNDER OF REACH10

"I was thrilled to find *Good Pictures Bad Pictures*. As a parent, it makes opening that sensitive conversation as easy and loving as reading a book together. I love everything about it! It's honest and open and calm and reassuring. What a beautiful way to empower and protect your child!"

DEANNA LAMBSON, MOTHER OF 6, TEACHER AND FOUNDER OF WHITERIBBONWEEK.ORG

"I highly recommend *Good Pictures Bad Pictures*. As I read this book to my children it opened up an opportunity to discuss difficult matters. It presents the material in a way that children can relate to and understand."

GREG, FATHER OF 6

"*Good Pictures Bad Pictures* is a book every family needs to read. It has been priceless in helping us start a dialogue with our young children about the harmful effects of pornography."

MARCIA STILLWELL, MOM OF 5

"Reading *Good Pictures Bad Pictures* with my children may be one of the most important things I've ever done for them. I have witnessed the ravaging effects of pornography in the lives of many loved ones, but until finding this book, I didn't know how to begin a dialogue with my young children to help neutralize pornography's powerful vortex of addiction. The book's meticulous word choice, powerful yet simple description of the two parts of the brain, and its "CAN DO" plan (the equivalent of a fire evacuation plan for any internet-enabled device) have given me tremendous peace of mind. I look forward to reinforcing its concepts often."

DIANE, MOTHER OF 6

TO MY HUSBAND, JOHN, WHOSE LOYALTY AND LOVE ENCOURAGE MY EVERY STEP.

—KRISTEN—

TO MY HUSBAND, STEVEN, WHO ALWAYS BELIEVES IN ME.

—DEBBIE—

Disclaimer

It is the opinion of the author that children are safer when they are proactively warned and empowered to reject the dangers of pornography and addiction. However, parents and caregivers are ultimately responsible for how they educate their children about these serious issues. This book does not constitute medical or psychological advice for treating addiction. People suffering from addiction should seek competent professional services.

INFO@GLENCOVEPRESS.COM

ISBN-10: 0-9973187-3-2

ISBN 13: 978-0-9973187-3-9

This book is available at quantity discounts.
For information, contact info@GlenCovePress.com

Book design by Evan MacDonald

Printed in the USA